DAITH HARDD

DAITH HARDD

Life, Love and the Beautiful Journey of

Finding My Authentic Self

Jennifer Gibson Joseph

This book is lovingly dedicated to Aziz.

She is me.

Author's Note

It all began as a simple experiment.

In August, 2012 I created a blog called Corff Hardd which was Welsh for Body Beautiful. For 30 days I refrained from looking at myself in the mirror in order to focus my attention on discovering what made me and you, beautiful. I needed to do this not only myself, but for my children. I wanted to include them in discussions and hear their thoughts on what they thought made a person beautiful. Nearly everyday of the experiment, I would post what both myself and my children had learned.

When the 30 days were complete, I knew there was still much more to learn about life, love and finding my authentic self. Thus, I created a "sister" blog called Daith Hardd which is Welsh for Beautiful Journey.

This book is exactly that. A beautiful journey. From my first, painful posts in September 2012 when I was struggling to keep my marriage afloat to being single and falling deeply in love with myself. The road was not always easy but writing on my blog always seemed to be a form of therapy and self reflection. I often found myself reviewing old posts and marvelling over how far I had come since those hard days in 2012.

Life is not to be endured, but rather enjoyed. My hope is that this will inspire others to truly begin their own Daith Hardd.

DAITH HARDD

CHAPTER ONE

The Fall

Lemonade

September 25, 2012

I named this blog similar to my other blog which was Corff Hardd - Welsh for Body Beautiful, this one being Daith Hardd - or Beautiful Journey. I try to be fairly positive person, viewing the world and its inhabitants as generally good rather than evil. Seeing the glass as being half full rather than half empty and if I should be handed lemons, I attempt to make lemonade. This blog is intended to celebrate all the beauty our senses allow us to, yet I haven't blogged in many days because I haven't been able to feel such emotions.

The truth, the UGLY truth, is that life sometimes isn't beautiful. Sometimes it's downright horrible. A nightmare. Total bullshit and I wish to either run from it, or bury myself deep under my covers. From past experiences, neither of those actually solve the problem(s) so I must just plod through the muck and not get stuck. This time I am stuck. As they say "Stuck between a rock and a hard place". I feel as though I have a decision to make, yet a decision really can't be made. I've made the proverbial pros/cons list and know what I should probably do, yet I can't. Sometimes decisions can't just be made by black/white or pros/cons list, sometimes those decisions are largely based on emotions, or emotions can at least confuse us.

I've heard friends say to me how they never imagined how certain events in their life would turn out or how they no longer recognize the person their loved one has become...I've listened and I've tried to be the supportive friend back, offering help if needed. Yet, I've never been able to really understand what it was they were talking about, that is until now. I'm at this crossroad and I'm confused and I'm scared and mostly, I'm heartbroken. I don't want to be HERE. I'm lost. THIS wasn't ever supposed to happen; it wasn't a part of the plan.

I'm trying to remain optimistic, and keep my sense of humour. I'm trying to laugh and crack jokes. I'm trying. I am really fucking trying. Yet, a song will come on or an old memory will pop up, or the old love letters...and then I feel sick to my stomach with sadness. I don't want any other person but him. Just him.

I'm leaving tomorrow (Wednesday, September 26) for a trip abroad for 2 weeks. I'll be traveling on my own, leaving my family with well cared for and capable hands. I'm excited beyond belief. I also won't be blogging often, if not even at all while I am away.

I'm running away from my troubles... but just temporarily

Until we meet again...If life gives you lemons, make a lemon daiquiri.

Daith Hardd

Home

October 15, 2012

"I live in my own little world. But it's ok, they know me here"
~ Lauren Myracle

I've returned home from one of the best vacations I've ever had. Spending time with good friends, plenty of rest and of course the beautiful ocean does wonders for one's soul. Near the end I was actually itching to get back to my "normal" life as wife/mother. I have arrived home.

How often do we take for granted what it is we have? As much as I was envious for those that lived near the sun and surf, I reminded myself of all the beauty that is offered here at home. The beautiful maple trees that I walk by on my way to take the children to school. The colours they change into during the autumn and the sap that makes maple syrup in the spring. We live 20 mins from the Oak Ridges Moraine which in the winter, attracts skiers/snowboarders for their snow covered hills. And in the summer, many families flock up north to Muskoka for the serene cottage and lake life. Yes, we are truly blessed with beauty in this country, yet so many times we fail to recognize what is right in front of our eyes.

Yes, so many times we fail to recognize the beauty that is right in front of us..

Daith Hardd

Bitter or Better?

November 28, 2012

I haven't been writing much these past few weeks, not for lack of topics but due to lack of energy. I'm heading back in with it today, although I can't promise what will come of it.

My girlfriend, to whom I talk to everyday, lives abroad and because of this we can't actually speak to each other on the phone easily so we text message one another instead. We're very much alike and yet very much different. She's my yang and I'm her ying. She's an atheist and I'm a theist. We enjoy a good debate and thought provoking conversations while always respecting each other's opinions.

Last week we ventured on the subject of happiness. Are we in charge of our own happiness or is it unattainable for some? Even through text messages, I could feel the heat from our differences of opinion come through. In fact, I think it might have been our most disagreeable conversation ever!

Are we in charge of our own happiness?

My most simple and straightforward answer is yes, but please let me explain. We as human beings have been given emotions...complex ones! I can easily rhyme off a dozen different emotions I've felt while watching a film or reading a book. Contentment, sadness, anger, grief, compassion, fear...Now beside those who suffer from mental health disorders, are we responsible for our emotions? Of course! I can't rob a bank and then blame it on the emotion of envy just like I can't assault someone due to uncontrollable rage. We are responsible for our emotions. We control our emotions, not the other way around.

So say you've been given a bum deal in life - and let's face it, there's always someone who has it harder than you, does that mean you're less deserving of happiness? Of course not! How many times have you heard of someone who has gone to hell and back and they are still able to smile and be thankful for the smallest of things?

I'm not saying that everyone should feel happy or appreciative of life when they've had it beyond tough. I'm also not saying that there isn't a time and place for anger, grief, and frustration. Nor am I trying to solve the world's problems with this blog post. But there comes a time when you have to choose which direction you want to take at the fork in the road. Bitter or Better. It's your life...even if someone takes everything you have; they can't take away your "joy".

Which takes me to an amazing painting of Bastogne, Belgium by Olin Dows in 1945. I was feeling down and deeply unhappy with some things that have been going on in my life when I happened to come across this painting. I started scrolling through many of the WWII pictures from the Battle of the Bulge and felt many, many emotions...it triggered the reminder in me that I am in charge my emotions and instead of thinking about all the negative that is happening around me, I focused on the positive. Sure, it's perfectly acceptable to feel the way I do, but I don't want to spend too much of my precious time focused on it. I want happiness and joy in my life, so I'm going to be introspective and pull it out.

Like I once heard, be bitter or better…it's your choice.

Daith Hardd

Misery Loves You

December 4, 2012

  Misery loves company.

Am I right? Of course I am. Just grab a newspaper or check out the latest news on CNN and tell me if I'm wrong. Miserable events tend to make up the bulk of the news these days. It's what we make small talk about and bring into our lives every single day. You'd have to live in the middle of nowhere in order to avoid it.

As if hearing and reading about others misery isn't enough, we might also have to endure our own share. I don't like dwelling or letting misery take a foothold in my life, but let's be realistic, it does happen. Sometimes I share my burdens with a few sweet souls but I have a hard time really opening up. I'll tell you why...judgement. I must explain that these lovely friends of mine would be hard pressed to actually judge anyone and yet I still don't want such to happen. If I have conflict with someone in my life, it means that they are important to me, and I don't wish for anyone to think poorly of them or me. A truly cathartic vent may feel good at the time, but the guilt afterward would far outweigh the good.

Who does one turn to at times of deep pain and frustration? Well for me it's the pen on paper route. Nothing quite feels as good as scratching that pain out onto a pure white sheet of paper. I fill it with all the foulest, descriptive language I have in me until there's nothing but chicken scratch and tears stains left. I re-read it. I add pieces that were left out on its first read, then I scribble more, slam my fist down on the God forsaken table, scrunch the papers into a ball and throw it into the fireplace.

At this point I'm tired and spent and need just one shot of vodka before calling it a night. Pen and paper has always made for better company and fire always keeps its secrets.

Misery loves company and yet I have no place for it.

Daith Hardd

I'm Still Breathing

December 6, 2012

I don't really know any of you, nor do you know me. I like this level of anonymity. I say what I have to say without fear of reprisal. Yet sometimes I still don't fully let loose. This will be short but sweet...something I just feel that needs to be said.

I'm young. I'm still living and breathing and I have desires. I never realized how important having a physical relationship was until I seemingly lost it. I was once chased, hounded and woken up to find loving and needy hands upon me. Now there is just an empty space between us. Sometimes I sneak over to his side just to listen to him quietly breath and I press my chest against his back to feel his warmth. That seems to be the only way I can get it.

I'm not looking for an affair or one night stand. I long for him. I want him to want me too. I want to connect physically and emotionally with him once again. I refuse to believe this is the end of our passion and our lovemaking.

I'm still living and breathing and waiting for you. Always.

Daith Hardd

Harvest

December 21, 2012

"Remember that children, marriages, and flower gardens reflect the kind of care they get."

H. Jackson Brown, Jr.

You reap what you sow. The effort you put into something will result in the appropriate reward. We've heard these quotes/sayings numerous times and we know them to be true. How can it not be? Makes perfect sense really. If we were to plant a seed and then walk away without any effort to give it the sunlight and water it needs to grow and thrive, it would perish. Same goes for a relationship. You can't give up if you wish to succeed.

There have been a few relationships in my life that I've had to let go or stop trying. Usually those ones have been results of numerous painful attempts at reconciliation where it was just deemed not possible and we moved on. Others though, require giving it all you've got and then some. One such relationship is my marriage.

Just like parenting, there is no marriage handbook given to you after you say your vows. You're newlyweds and its considered the "honeymoon period" where life as a couple is blissful. You're excited to come home from work just to spend time with your partner. Doing mundane activities seems to be more fun while they're with you. You can't imagine the love you have for one another will ever fade and yet slowly it does. You may begin to fight more over small and insignificant things or you may do the opposite, become silent. Either way, both are painful and result in more deterioration of the marriage.

So what do we do about this? Well we nurture our relationship by either getting advice through friends/family, marriage therapy or finding an appropriate book. Remembering that we reap what we sow...even if that means our partner isn't, because sometimes it takes our first move to get the ball rolling.

I had a hard time struggling with this. I felt as though I was doing all the giving and I was receiving nothing in return. I felt as though maybe it was better if I just quit. Maybe if I gave into my emotions, I might find happiness elsewhere…but I had more questions.

Are my emotions controlling me or am I in control of my emotions? Are my emotions right or are my morals? Here's what I decided. As good as it may feel to leave my current situation I would be hurting those around me. I'm no martyr and I'm not saying that this is what everyone else should do. What I do know is that, I'm going to keep trying. I'm going to keep positive. I'm going to nourish this relationship until it blooms into my biggest reward.

Daith Hardd

CHAPTER TWO

The Spring

New Beginnings…Sakura

May 1, 2013

"Break open a cherry tree and there are no flowers, but the spring breeze brings forth myriad blossoms"

~Ikkyu Sojun

Spring gives birth to new beginnings. Maybe the timing is significant with the changes that have happened over the winter period or as I like to call it, my hibernation. I had plenty of time to stay indoors and think about the coming year and what changes were to be made in my personal life. As much as I wanted to write and get my feelings out on paper, I couldn't actually put a single word down - I'm still struggling now it seems. So instead of writing sad and depressing nonsense, I decided to leave it be and sort things out before I made another post.

It's now been sorted.

My husband and I are separating. We've been best of friends for 16 years and would have been celebrating our 10th year of marriage this coming August. I think we've both known for the last few years that we had matured and grown apart but neither of us wanted to admit it. We have two young children and that was the main bonding that kept us from parting ways years ago. This decision wasn't made lightly or easily but either way, the decision has been made and set in motion.

I'm still rusty at writing since it's been a few month but the only way to get back into the swing of things, is to get back into the swing of things!! Its spring...nearly summer. Time to be reborn, new beginnings! This is the most beautiful time of year for the Cherry Blossom tree (my absolute favourite) or Sakura. The Japanese pay close attention to the flower forecast and turn out in large numbers at parks, shrines, and temples with family and friends to hold flower-viewing parties. To sit and enjoy a beautiful picnic underneath such a gorgeous cloud of flowers... blissful

As painful as a time this is for both of us, we have both expressed how there is a sense of relief in finally admitting the truth. Now is the time for both of us to grow, bloom and grab love and life with both hands.

Be sure to do the same.

Daith Hardd

Land of Fire And Ice

May 27, 2013

"Begin at once to live, and count each separate day as a separate life."

~Seneca

A new chapter of my life has now begun and I finally feel as though I am flourishing. Its been quite the journey arriving at this point and I am thankful for every painful step that I had to take to arrive here. I'm now able to truly focus on discovering who I am, what I want out of this life and how else I can make a positive impact on those around me.

I've always been more of a follower, never one to lead. I've counted on many other to do this for me and now I am having to stand on my own two feet and chart my own path. It's exciting, exhilarating and also terrifying...but I won't let that stop me.

My first step after the dust has settled with my separation/divorce is to go on my very own dream vacation...and I'm doing it on my own. I've traveled on my own twice to Australia but it was always to visit my best friend where she did a fantastic job at playing host. Both of those trips helped prepare me for this next one: Iceland, the land of fire and ice.

I've always had a love affair with the Nordic countries over all other hot, tropical destinations. One of the reasons might very well be because they have few insect species (I nearly left OZ after my second day there due to a wrestling match with a Huntsman spider) but of course there is much more to offer than that little perk. I love nature and the outdoors and in my opinion, Iceland is the perfect destination for me. Dramatic landscapes, wilderness, picturesque mountains, stunning views of waterfalls and brooks, hiking, camping... I could go on and on. I want to experience the majesty of Iceland on my own, focusing on simply MYSELF.

Live your life. Be happy, its a beautiful journey

Daith Hardd

Yin Yang

June 4, 2013

You either feel it or you don't. Writing that is. When the timing is right, you quite literally have to put everything else down and spend time getting what's on your mind out onto paper. So, here I am...

Yin and Yang. Hot and cold. Light and dark. Male and female. All of these are natural dualities which seemingly have contrary forces when in fact they are complementary, not opposing forces, interacting to form a whole greater than either separate part. Everything has both yin and yang aspects, for example shadow cannot exist without light... I'm currently working through both feelings of elation and somber.

My life is amazing. I have very little to complain about. I'm at peace and happy with who I am and enjoy my own company. I have wonderful, loving friends and family who I do my very best not to take for granted. I wake up each morning excited to start my day and learn or meet someone new. I'm happy. I feel it inside...content and joyful. So how is it that while feeling such beautiful emotions I still have a nagging heart sickness? It's really pissing me off.

How can I have ALL that I have and yet still feel this ridiculous sense of sadness? I know the answer. I want a connection with the opposite sex. I'm happy to wake up and spend some solitude time walking at the lake or meeting up with girlfriends for wine and conversation. I enjoy reading, writing, quiet contemplation. I am happy exploring life on my own but I realize that my heart longs to be connected with another for a much deeper relationship than I could ever have with myself.

I'm picky. I know what I want and what I don't want. I've felt that amazing connection and I have no desire to look for it elsewhere. I wonder if that was the one that I'll always long for and be forever thinking about? Will I eventually just settle or will I find someone just as amazing or better?

I can't answer these question and obviously neither can any of you, so in the mean time, punch me in the heart and kick me in the crotch...Its the only way to knock some sense into me.

In the mean time,

Daith Hardd

Love

June 7, 2013

Here is what I know. I have love. Over flowing love that I feel fortunate enough to share with all those that I come into contact with. Don't ask me to describe why that is, it simply is. This brings me such deep joy and happiness.

I love. I hope this never leaves me. I hope to carry it with me and pass it on to you all. Love is all around us if we are only to open our eyes and let it in. You can find it in the arts, sciences, our amazing earth and heavens...in those we meet, pass and have to opportunity to build relationships with.

Love is what we all deserve and desire and it can be yours. We are taught to love ourselves which is easier said than done but I urge you all to take the time to do such. Everyday love yourself and everyday you will be able to give it freely to those around you. Love every moment of your existence and pass it on. Look to the good in others. See them as beautiful extensions of yourself. Love. It is all around us, resides in us and is absolutely intoxicatingly magical.

Enough of the lecture. Go. Love.

Daith Hardd

Sabbatical

June 7, 2013

"At the center of your being you have the answer; you know who you are and you know what you want." ~Lao Tzu

Sabbatical.

A time when one takes a break from their career in order to complete research, finish writing a book, travelling or as I am doing, finding myself. I'm not actually taking time off from work to do this but I am stepping away from social media such as Twitter so that I can best channel my efforts accordingly.

My proverbial "Bucket List" of things I wish to do in this lifetime has become neglected and needs my undivided attention in order to really start experiencing and checking things off. This is truly a vacation of the mind, body and soul for me.

For my mind, knowledge is power. I have a list of books and articles that I plan on immersing myself in, while enjoying a beer and soaking up the sun. Moral Origins: The evolution of virtue, altruism and shame by Christopher Boehm has been looking at me for more than a year. I'm rather giddy to finally pick it up and soak up his words.

For my body, there will be movement. Walking, hiking, dancing and anything that can create the intoxicating release of endorphins. Being able to do all of these things outside in the country that I love while being surrounded by such beauty is nothing short of amazing.

For my soul, spiritual enlightenment. I'm a theist. I believe in a higher power, a God that loves me unconditionally and wants me to love others the same. I plan on taking these next few months exploring other religions and beliefs. The more we learn, the more love, compassion, humility and thankfulness we can experience and pass on to others.

I never want to stop growing, learning and experiencing what this life has to offer. I'm mindful that at any moment my time may be called and because of this, I want lead a good and love filled life.

Daith Hardd

Perspective

June 24, 2013

"The glass is not empty. It is waiting for you to fill it with whatever you chose."

It's all a matter of perspective, isn't it? The proverbial glass half empty, half full argument has now taken a whole new dimension with those stating that technically it has always been full...half air, half water. I like this new perspective. Life isn't always black and white, sometimes it's a murky grey with a dash of column A and column B. Hell, sometimes it changes from day to day.

A few weeks ago a friend sent me the story of the Taoist Farmer. I was having one of those really emotional moments when all that came out of my mouth were loud sobs and my eyes were so puffy I could barely see out of them and the last thing I wanted to do was read this long parable. I'm not going to try and say that after reading it, I had this huge soul awakening moment, in fact I felt nothing. Two days later I went back to the story and re-read it over and over and over. Let me share with you this parable.

The Story of the Taoist Farmer

This farmer had only one horse, and one day the horse ran away. The neighbours came to console over his terrible loss. The farmer said, "What makes you think it is so terrible?"

A month later, the horse came home--this time bringing with her two beautiful wild horses. The neighbours became excited at the farmer's good fortune. Such lovely strong horses! The farmer said, "What makes you think this is good fortune?"

The farmer's son was thrown from one of the wild horses and broke his leg. All the neighbours were very distressed. Such bad luck! The farmer said, "What makes you think it is bad?"

A war came, and every able-bodied man was conscripted and sent into battle. Only the farmer's son, because he had a broken leg, remained. The neighbours congratulated the farmer. "What makes you think this is good?" said the farmer.

Sometimes what we perceive to be absolutely horrible at the time turns out to be a exactly what we needed. Those hard times shape us into who we are and show us how we can triumph over adversity. You almost have to learn to just roll with things, be more fluid and not get all bent out of shape either way. Easier said than done of course.

I printed that story and tucked it into my purse. It's a good reminder for me to not have to decide if the glass is half full, half empty or filled with a bunch of hot air.

Daith Hardd

Clarity

July 4, 2013

Simplicity, clarity, singleness: These are the attributes that give our lives power and vividness and joy as they are also the marks of great art. They seem to be the purpose of God for his whole creation.

~Richard Holloway

Clarity is more than just a feeling. There's an emotional state associated with it, but it's more than that. Clarity is a certain vibe. When you're really clear, you can sense that vibe through every cell of your being. Your mind and emotions are centered. Every part of you is on the same page. There's no doubt of uncertainty. This is a powerful state of being to experience.

It's very easy to get lost in the mental process of trying to achieve mental clarity in the hussle and bussle of life. Life can be a complicated affair, overwhelming for many and at some time or another we all face questions like:

"What is my purpose in life?"

"How do I navigate through this difficult decision?"

"What is my next step?"

"What if I make the wrong decision?"

From experience, I've often found myself getting caught up in the endless cycle of incessant thinking, calculating, worrying and second guessing my way through my troubles. None of which have helped other than to create more questions and painful headaches. At my most desperate moments I've even thrown my dilemma at a friend to give me the final answer.

How is it that some people just seem to have that certain CLARITY in every single life choice they make? Life is a beautiful story with no antagonist to confront or overcome. Nothing fazes them. They are completely zen with the world.

These traits may not come naturally to me but I have found a few helpful ways in order to achieve more clarity.

<u>1. Pick one goal/question to sort out at a time.</u>

Too many goals will have you bouncing around, unable to focus and ultimately make little progress on any of them. Instead, focus on just the one until it is achieved.

<u>2. Pay attention to the journey, not just the end result.</u>

Sometimes the way you achieve a particular goal is more important than the goal itself. Self discovery is always fun and exciting so don't be afraid to take the scenic route.

<u>3. You have control over your life outcomes.</u>

Whether good or bad, you are the one who must adjust outside influences in order to achieve your goals. Rarely are the moments of clarity accidental. If you want clarity all the time, you must practice it just like you would anything else.

4. Get busy creating clarity.

Don't wait for clarity to come to you. You are responsible for creating it within so when you're stuck in a state of ambivalence, do whatever it takes to break the impasse. Doing what you're already doing won't get you anywhere so try something radically different in your approach. Write down some plans on how to achieve these goals but also get moving. Standing still will get you nowhere fast.

These are just a few tips that I've used in the past to make important decisions, large or small. The more I practice them, the easier my life becomes. What I do know is that clarity isn't something that arrives from outside to you. Clarity isn't a matter of luck either. Clarity is what you create for yourself. It is a decision. Whatever degree of clarity you're experiencing right now is what you've decided to create. Not deciding still counts as a decision; in that case it's the decision to remain uncertain.

Until then,

Daith Hardd

Diotima

July 8, 2013

"Diotima, a wise woman from Mantinea, is the one who taught me the art of love."

~Socrates

From Plato's Symposium

Life is a beautiful journey, or as they say in Welsh, daith hardd. That's what the focus of this blog has been about from the very beginning. My journey, my thoughts and the lessons I've learned along the way.

I'm never without questions and therefore I'm often busy looking for answers, most of which are open to interpretation. Love is often a theme of mine. What is love? What purpose does it serve? What does it look like? Like many philosophical questions, there is more than one answer.

In pursuit of these answers I found myself intrigued by the thoughts of Plato, specifically his philosophical text. In this, Love is examined during a drinking party in which each male gives a speech in praise of love and how they interpret it. Their views on Love vary from one guest giving a very comedic speech while another offering a much more sombre, tragic viewpoint. Near the end of the party, Plato offers us Socrates speech which is the most memorable and insightful of the group.

Socrates relays what he has learned from his teacher, the great priestess Diotima. Diotima explains to Socrates that there is much more to the mysteries of love than simply the desire that exists between two human beings. She explains to Socrates that as we progress in our lives we grow in our conception of love. First we are stirred by the beauty of the young body. Then we begin to see the beauty in all bodies. At this point we look to the beauty of the soul. As man is able to identify the beauty in all souls, he soon appreciates the beauty in the laws, and the structure of all things. Lastly, we discover the beauty of the forms, the divine ideas. Love is important for it starts and continues us on our path.

Diotima suggests that one can approach the truth of Love's mysteries only through a slow and careful ascent. This can be viewed as the Ladder of Love where one can progress from rung to rung from the beauties of the flesh to the loving pure beauty, truth and goodness.

Plato's "Ladder of Love"-The Ascent to Beauty Itself

1. <u>Beauties of the body</u> - the most obvious form of love, natural and easy to do and therefore the lowest rung on the ladder.

2. <u>Beauty in all bodies</u> - recognizing that all bodies are relatively similar and that the beauty contained in this beautiful body is not original. To get to the second rung you

"must consider how nearly related the beauty of any one body is the beauty of any other". Diotima explains to Socrates that soon you will be the lover of every lovely body and see that the single body you loved first isn't all that unique.

3. <u>Beauty of the soul</u> - appreciating the beauty of the mind/soul, regardless of their physical beauty. You "must grasp that the beauties of the body are as nothing to the beauties of the soul". As you climb the ladder you discover "every kind of beauty is akin to every other, and he will conclude that the beauty of the body is not, after all, of so great moment."

4. <u>Beauty of the laws</u> - at this point you'll see the beauty in many things, even in institutions and abstractions such as human rights and justice. That which is responsible for their existence; a moderate harmonious and just social order.

5. <u>Beauty of knowledge</u> - Diotima shows us that knowledge is found in many ways. We gain access to some through our perceptions, our senses. Some knowledge is reached through insight, the mind.

6. <u>Beauty itself</u> - This is not a particular thing that is beautiful, but is instead the very essence of beauty or Love. Ultimately, this lover of knowledge will reach the goal of love, which is amazingly beautiful in it's nature. This beauty always exists, not coming into being or ceasing to be, not increasing or diminishing. It is absolute beauty, not being beautiful only in some respects or at some times or in relation to certain things or in certain places or to certain people. Beauty will not appear

in certain bodies or in certain forms of knowledge or anywhere in particular: it will appear in itself and by itself, independent of everything else. All beautiful things share in its character, but these things in no way effect Beauty itself.

Diotima explains to Socrates that by going through these stages, one will ascend from loving particular kinds of beauty to loving Beauty itself, from which all beautiful things derive their nature. She explains that a life gazing upon and pursuing this Beauty is the best life one can lead. Those who are obsessed with images of beauty can only produce images of virtue, but those who can see Beauty itself can produce virtue itself, making themselves immortal and loved by the gods. Socrates concludes that ever since speaking with Diotima he has known that there is no greater partner for human nature than Love.

Working my way through Plato's Ladder of Love has been a truly exciting and enlightening experience. Having Love broken down into such a simplistic manner while also being extremely complex is nothing short of amazing. You start by a natural love for the beauties of the flesh and end up loving pure beauty, truth and goodness.

Love is a journey, a beautiful journey - Daith Hardd!

We Are In This Together

August 8, 2013

"I speak of a clinical depression that is the background of your entire life, a background of anguish and anxiety, a sense that nothing goes well, that pleasure is unavailable and all your strategies collapse."

~Leonard Cohen"

It doesn't comes easy. Positivity. It takes practice, daily commitment and motivation to change your thought pattern. I can say this because I've been down the dark and painful road of depression and although I'm not "cured", I manage it quite well. Let me give you the Coles notes version.

I had a pretty good childhood...typical ups and downs and a few curve balls, but let's face it, no one's life is perfect. My parents divorced when I was a toddler and I lived with my mother until I was 14 when I experienced my first bout of depression. I moved in with my father, talked it out with a psychologist and eventually found my footing again.

Fast forward 13 years...I nearly died from it this time.

I had just given birth to my second child, a very dramatic and awful experience that completely wiped me out physically and emotionally. Within two weeks of giving birth I had become paranoid, unable to sleep and eventually decided to end it all. Fortunately, I had family who reacted quickly and I was then hospitalized for 6 weeks to sort medication/treatment out. I should have been terrified of the company I was around, but I was so numb that I welcomed being away from my "life" as it stood. three times a week for nearly three weeks I had ECT (Electro-convulsive therapy - or as some know of it as "shock therapy") which sort of re-wired my depressive brain to better working order. I also took part in group therapy, workshops and found the proper medication for myself.

I am living proof that you can not only survive depression, but THRIVE.

I'm stable. I take my medication daily and will do so for the rest of my life and because I am stable and able to think/see things clearly, I can make the decision to change how I view the world. At first, just trying to see the positive in my life was a challenge, but I persevered. Each day I woke up, I would remind myself to find at least one bright ray of sunshine and write it down. Slowly, I found I was able to end my day with a list of all the great and amazing things that had happened to me until eventually, I woke up and didn't have to "find" things to be thankful for...they simply found me.

I've been working on this positivity project/life journey for 5 years now and it hasn't always been easy (as you may have seen from all my previous blog postings). I try and surround myself and seek out the good things/people. I try and see others points of view. I try to find the good in people. The key is that I TRY...most of the times I succeed but there are still times that I don't, and I'm ok with this.

So please, don't think for a moment that I'm just trying to stuff all these good vibe tweets on twitter or my blog, down your throat...I genuinely care about your mental health and happiness. Whether we want to believe it or not, we are all in this crazy life together...directly or indirectly...so lets make it a beautiful journey.

Daith Hardd

Give, Receive and Evolve

August 14, 2013

"Without continual growth and progress, such words as improvement, achievement, and success have no meaning. ~Benjamin Franklin"

I'm an only child and because of this, I've often found myself to be a bit more mature from those of the same age. My choice in music, fashion and conversation has always stood me apart from my peers. I remember trying to fit in with the music crowd in my teenage years, yet having no clue what songs belonged to which artist. I dreaded the goofy questions kids would ask one another, "What type of music do you like?" or "Who's your favourite band?". Sure, I could easily answer those questions but truth be told, it would only make me stand out as more of a misfit than I already was. I distinctly remember buying Notorious B.I.G. when every ounce of me wanted to order Sade. My girlfriend still teases me about learning the lyrics to Big Poppa.

I know why I did a lot of these things - to fit in, to belong, to blend in...to disappear. As much as I wanted to be apart of the cool crowd, I also wanted to stay off their radar. It was like walking on eggshells. Wanting to be accepted just as you are but knowing that it could be used as a weapon against you. I can recall countless times when I was humiliated and tormented by the very same people that I thought had it all. Popular, good looking, smart...none of the traits I had - I was simply known as Jenn, the goofy (sometimes funny), shy girl that no one paid any attention to unless it was to have a laugh.

Those years were extremely hard to navigate through and I honestly don't think I could go back and do it again. Yet if I hadn't experienced them, I wouldn't be who I am today...and I like who I am. Through cruelty I learned about compassion. Those who were arrogant pointed me to become humble just as those that were judgemental taught me to be more tolerant. These are life lessons that I couldn't have learned unless I had experienced them.

I still want to fit in with crowd, but I'm no longer willing to sacrifice my character in order to do so. You could say I've become more mellow and less opinionated than I was when I knew everything at the ripe old age of 20. I'm putting my foot less and less in my mouth and opening my ears to other points of views. I no longer see things as right or wrong because there is a lot of in-betweens and I am guilty of skewing the lines. I've done things that I'm not proud of, I've made big mistakes but I'm gaining wisdom each time.

The journey to get here has been a long, painful one but that's the beauty of life, learning from your experiences and passing it along to others. Are we not all a work in progress?

Give and receive and remember it's a Daith Hardd.

Strong Women

August 26, 2013

I've always been attracted to women who are strong in character, intelligent and independent. They radiate self-confidence and its hard not to be drawn near to them. That's how I would describe my circle of friends. Incredibly amazing, fierce women who I consider my big sisters. They take the role in stride, keeping me safely under their guidance and always looking out for me. I've often compared myself to being their "little sister" due to the fact that I can be a bit naive and not as grounded as them. Things are starting to change...in the best possible way.

There has to be a balance in life. Everything in moderation as they say. These ladies have it down pat and have been trying to rub their ways off on me for years, and I'm finally listening to their advice.

They're realists. They don't romanticize things or hope for the best. They look ahead and plan and they're sure to protect their heart in the process. I've often been sitting and discussing things with them and their advice would fall on my deaf ears. I would defend my actions to them by saying some positive/ hippy jargon, truly believing my own BS. Them being such amazing friends, would simply listen and tell me that if I needed to talk they would be there for me. Never any pressure that I had to do what they were advising me to do. They just wanted to look out and protect me.

So I've finally pulled my head out of the clouds (or maybe even out of my own ass) and started truly listening to them. I've decoded what they have been saying for years... It's ok to be kind, positive and compassionate but you also need to be prepared for the "worst case" scenarios. I need to be a realist. I need to focus on myself and my children rather than worrying about the other person.

Of course I'm still the same goofy, happy Jenn but I think I'm really gaining the confidence/strength that my friends always had and wanted me to have too. I'm becoming independent. Assertive. These are huge strides for me and I'm so thankful I have such amazing friends who see the potential in me, even when I didn't. I still view them as my "big sisters" and I hope I'm making them proud.

Remember, it's a Daith Hardd

We Will Flourish

August 27, 2013

"What greater aspiration and challenge are there for a mother than the hope of raising a great son or daughter?" ~ Rose Kennedy

I was laying with my daughter last night, listening to a song on repeat and rubbing her back. She's a music lover like myself and she's happy to have quiet time with me, daydreaming until she falls asleep. Every now and again she would ask me a question that had popped into her mind, seemingly from out of nowhere.

Lily's my anxious girl. She's quiet, shy and very thoughtful but almost to a fault. I did a blog post approx a year ago on my original blog Corff Hardd (30 Days to Self Love) about our struggles with her. She was diagnosed with General Anxiety Disorder (GAD) a little over a year ago. Below is a brief description of GAD:

"Generalized anxiety disorder (GAD) is an anxiety disorder that is characterized by excessive, uncontrollable, unexplained and often irrational worries about everyday things that are disproportionate to the actual source of worry. This excessive worry often interferes with daily functioning, as individuals suffering GAD typically anticipate disaster, and are overly concerned about everyday matters"

Of course this isn't the end of the world, we all have some sort of stress or anxiety in our life that we have to battle and that's exactly how I handle things with Lily. She's come an incredibly long way since her diagnosis but she still has her challenges. I'm conscious that I have to be careful on how I approach certain subjects with her or how she will interpret my actions. I try to protect her but I have to tread lightly - protecting can easily create more problems and more irrational fears.

She's wise and she knows something is wrong with our family unit. We've been good at keeping them safe from knowing the truth as it stands right now but we both fear how Lily will react to things. I'm still angry that she can't be spared from this. Angry that I've been put in a situation that has made me have to choose. My children's happiness has been the driving force for most of my life decisions and right now, I'm not doing what they need. They need two parents, one home and love. I just shake my head that this has happened, this is my new life.

Onward and upward though. They need me to be strong and to help them navigate their emotions during this difficult time. Lily will survive, as will Jonah and I truly believe this. I have the tools I need to assist Lily, I'll pay special attention to Jonah so that he's not overlooked and I'll keep plugging along. We will all flourish.

It's a Daith Hardd

If You Can Do This…

August 28, 2013

If you can do this, then you can do anything. I look back and laugh, but it was the honest truth. I was 24 and my husband was going away for 3 months and I needed a reliable car. Being as cheap as I am, I decided that in order to save a few dollars I would purchase a manual transmission and simply learn how to drive it. Easy enough is what I thought.

So we went and picked up the car from the dealership and my husband drove me over to the empty parking lot near our home. I got in, adjusted my seat, put my foot on the clutch, started her up and then just as quickly I stalled it. I spent an hour just trying to get used to starting the car and getting it into first gear. My husband was patient but of course I was becoming more and more anxious as the minutes went by. He was leaving in just a few days and if I didn't learn how to drive this car, I'd be walking to work and everywhere else I needed to go…not only that, but I'd be paying for a car that I couldn't drive. Frustrated and full of tears, I told him I'd had enough for the day and wanted to go home.

What was I thinking? Why would I buy a new car without even knowing how to drive manual transmission? What kind of idiot was I? Just to save a few bucks I had gotten myself into this huge mess and the worst part was that my husband would be leaving in just three days, leaving me with no other means of transportation. I remember crying myself to sleep that night.

The next morning it really hit me. I was so used to knowing that whenever I got into any kind of jam, I had family and friends who would readily bail me out – this time it was different – I literally had to grow up and be a big girl. I had to learn how to drive this freaking car, no excuses. I still remember telling myself this corny line, "Jenn, if you learn how to drive this car, you will be able to do anything". No joke, honest truth.

I'm sure it's probably quite the silly story to hear or imagine – that simply learning how to drive a manual transmission could give someone the confidence they didn't have in themselves prior, but it's true. I would get up early, give myself plenty of time to get to work and then take the quietest roads to get there. I stalled it plenty of times, often with many other cars behind me, but I was on my own and I had to figure it out FAST. I would wait until it was late at night, around 10pm and then practise getting into first gear while on a hill – the most terrifying part of learning manual in my opinion. I did all this while my husband was hours away. I couldn't rely on him, I had to rely on myself and obviously I managed just fine. I'm a pro at driving manual transmission and I'm so proud of myself for sticking with it and believing in myself. It sounds completely ridiculous, but that experience taught me a lot about myself. That I'm not a quitter. That I can rely on myself. That I can do anything.

So this brings me to where I am right now and no joke, I still think about that learning experience and remind myself of what I said nearly 10 years ago – if you can do this, you can do anything … I CAN do anything.

Enjoy the journey, it's a Daith Hardd

The Anniversary

August 29, 2013

10 years ago today I was married to my best friend. We were married on a Friday, at a small church with just our parents in attendance. Instead of spending thousands on a wedding, we saved the money to put a down payment on our first home. He wore a pinstripe suit and I wore an off white skirt suit. It was low key, no fuss, in other words, perfect.

In the past 10 years we have accomplished a lot. We both have successful careers, a home, hobbies, friends and of course two amazing children. We've been best friends laughing at each other's jokes, finishing each other's sentences and a great parenting team. Lots of laughter and few tears but most of all, an incredible journey.

Today has been bittersweet for me. I spent most of the morning tired, miserable and just wanting to go back to bed. I found myself clenching my teeth and biting my lower lip as I often do when I get stressed or really pissed off. I was essentially punishing myself with this sort of behavior and what for? Do I get a reward for wallowing in my own misery? Absolutely not. I'm tired of fighting and arguing with another person, let alone myself.

Instead, I'm going to celebrate the good memories we had with a bit of whiskey, probably a few teary phone calls to girlfriends and then fall asleep to some romantic, corny song.

It's going to be good and fine and all that jazz.

Daith Hardd

Next Chapter

September 1, 2013

Except for our very close friends/family, the news of our separation came as a huge surprise to others. We've never had public feuds or not been seen having a good time with each other, so when we started sharing the news, people just couldn't understand why we couldn't make it work. What they didn't realize is that we had tried to make it work. We had put in hours of therapy with a handful of different therapist, talked to other long married couples to find out their secrets and yet we still couldn't make our marriage last. Without going into the personal details of what our marriage was lacking, I can easily say we had one of the strongest friendships going.

Why does any of this matter now? Well for one reason, we have two incredible children that we need to co-parent and for another reason, separating while remaining friends is that much easier. We trust each other when it comes to the financial matters, custody arrangements and overall fairness toward each other. I still enjoy hanging out with him and doing things as a family - even if things are a new kind of "family".

I'm struggling with losing my friend. Living together had it's own set of difficulties but living apart is also difficult. Having that friend to share the eye rolls with when the children say something unknowingly funny, cracking each other up with jokes about our day, exchanging idea's or debating current events, hanging out to watch a favourite show or movie... I'm not complaining, I know how incredibly fortunate our situation is but give me some slack, i'm still allowed to mourn what once was.

I know in the future things are going to change and we'll have to navigate that carefully. One of us will start dating and we'll have to respect those new boundaries. I'd like to think we'll be cheering each other on, but more than likely it will hurt and sting...no way around it really.

For now, we have our ups and downs but our friendship remains. I'm still high fiving his dinner creations and he's still laughing at my awful jokes. How can something so positive and easy be so damn hard?

Daith Hardd

My Brain on Math

September 5, 2013

"Pure mathematics is, in its way, the poetry of logical ideas"
~Albert Einstein

Mathematical thinking, that's what I call my thought process. Now, I don't actually go around reciting Pi or anything of the sort but my mind is always questioning or problem solving something. I'm intrigued by life, nature, astronomy and the sciences. Something as simple as watching the clouds float by makes my brain buzz with activity. I find myself trying to sort out the why's and how's on any given subject, often wishing I could pick the brain of others.

There's no off switch for my magical brain so my only reprieve is listening to music or reading books. I recently came upon a book by Daniel Tammet called Thinking in Numbers : On life, love, meaning and math. I'm by no means anywhere near as brilliant as this man, but I could absolutely relate to his love for math. He brought colour, texture and emotions to numbers that I had always known existed but never found someone to put it down on paper. It all sounds rather mad, and maybe you have to be a bit crazy to love the subject. To see the world as a puzzle or a game. Asking questions that don't have a particularly correct answer.

I wish to quiet my mind at times. I'm fidgety by nature, always shaking my leg when its crossed, tapping my fingers, twirling my hair, moving in some way or another. So it seems only natural that my thoughts are in constant motion as well. On my own I sit and read articles in the news, which then takes me to looking up a definition when I become perplexed, ultimately leading me to an entirely different subject altogether. Bouncing around and frustratingly enough, never fully digesting whatever it is I read.

So where the heck am I going with all this? Well, deeper than any physical relationship could give me, I need a soulful, mindful, heartfelt connection. Someone who I can sit up and talk to all night with nothing physical happening. Someone who will listen to my oddball questions and come back with some of their own. Someone who simply by conversation can excite me. The mind is so magical and when you connect on that level, every physical touch can be explosive.

Only then will my mind become quiet.

Daith Hardd

Melancholy

September 10, 2013

<u>Melancholy</u>

There are times when I feel painfully alone.

I despise my own company,

The darkness of my thoughts.

No one desires to keep

company of the melancholy.

Yet I am forced to play

Happy host to these shameful

emotions.

I seek no pity or condolences,

Just acceptance

To be who I am, comfortable

In my own skin

Finding joy in my solitude

Daith Hardd

Reykjavik, Here We Come!

September 16, 2013

As many of you know, I have been preparing for my dream vacation to Iceland and I've finally booked my flight. I'll be leaving in the middle of February and meeting up with my girlfriend on Thursday morning in Reykjavik. We'll be staying for 5 days and we plan on jam packing as much as possible into that time.

Iceland is the type of place that you really need to go back and visit more than once. First of all, the adventure you can experience in the winter months vary from those that you can enjoy in the summer. I have a list of places I want to go and see and now I'm trying to sort out how I can make it all happen at a good price point and in accordance with our agenda. So much to organize and plan for and I'm enjoying every minute of it.

I'm in no hurry to rush the time along leading up to my big trip, it will go by fast enough. It's simply nice knowing that I've purchased my flight and I have something to look forward to during this tough time in my life. I'm even more pleased knowing that my girlfriend is joining me. I enjoy my own company, but having a sidekick to chat, laugh and drink with will top it all off. She's my soul sister in many ways and I'm beyond excited to experience this amazing trip with her.

Iceland truly is a Daith Hardd!!

The Next Time

September 18, 2013

The next time I fall in love, you'll fall first. I will protect my heart with armour, a fortress that cannot be penetrated by words. Your actions -thoughtful, kind and tender will be the only way to win my heart.

The next time I fall in love I will reserve a part of my heart just for me. A sacred spot that will always love it's owner. Somewhere that I can always lean and trust upon. True love will be first and foremost with myself.

The next time I fall in love, I will stay true to who I am. I will be strong and confident. I'll have difference of opinion than yours and you'll love me even more for it. You'll never ask me to change because you'll know I don't need to.

The next time I fall in love it will be with a man who is equally smitten with me as I am of him. He'll never tire of laying next to me at night. Of silently holding my hand while listening to music. Of falling in love with each other over and over again....

Daith Hardd

Languages of Love

September 20, 2013

The man is an Adonis. There's not an inch of him I didn't absolutely love. His hands are that of an artist and yet unmistakably masculine. Bronzed, broad shoulders that draw my gaze in and then lead them toward a perfectly sculpted chest. Long legs that are both lean and muscular from years of competitive sports. One look onto his face and I'm hooked. The most beautiful lips, eyes and yes, nose you've ever seen.

He's a man's man. He drinks beer, hunts, plays sports and smokes cigars. He respects women and appreciates the female form. He loves a woman in high heels. He can cook, entertain guests and loves the arts. He's intelligent, confident, down to earth and never boastful.

Emotions are his weakness and we don't speak the same language of love. I'm passionate with the world and I'm generous with my feelings. To touch, a hand on another or a hug, I freely give to those I encounter. Words, spoken or expressed, show that I care. He on the other hand is more stoic and practical with how he feels. His proof of devotion are through his good works and deeds. We clashed, repelled one another by our difference in the language of love...

Daith Hardd

Bleakness

September 25, 2013

It's creeping in. The black cloud that usually greets me and takes up residence somewhere between January and March. Depression.

I've noticed the signs for a few weeks now but it's finally settled in and made itself comfortable. The dreaded worm that seeks out the tiniest of holes to permeate my brain and twist my thoughts. Draining my energy and happiness along with it. Consuming me, bit by tiny bit.

I feel as though I have hands squeezing my neck, allowing only a whimper to get through. Occasionally they loosen up in which my body lets out the loudest howl of pain and misery. Screams that run through my body like electricity, shooting out of my fingers and toes and hot tears that always accompany it.

Anxious and nauseous. Both symptoms that are always at the surface, every single day for the past three weeks. I'm afraid. Absolutely terrified of not having my best friend/Husband in my life. I might vomit just writing this. It's right at the back of my throat…the urge to purge and run the hell away from my life.

It doesn't matter if you're a good person or a bad person. You're just a person and shit happens. This is an epic storm of such and I'm trying to come to terms with it. I know I will, it's a process and a journey and there's really no other choice but to get through it.

But I'm in a lot of pain. A lot.

Daith Hardd

Driving

September 30, 2013

"Come on Sport, let's go for a drive". That's the nickname my dad called me for most of my younger years, that and McGillicuddy. I'm an only child and growing up I always thought my dad wished I had been born a boy. He'd buy me Transformers for Christmas or remote control trucks for my birthday, nothing of which this little girl wanted. I remember visiting him and wrapping my remote control truck in a blanket, carrying it around like it was the doll I so wished he would have given me. So being called "Sport" was completely normal and even a bit endearing for me.

He had a boat of a car back in the 80's, as did everyone. It was his prize - waxed up in all its maroon glory that he affectionately called Betsy. We'd get in the car, I'd sit on a pillow in the front seat and head out for one of his quiet drives. He'd just drive, sometimes the radio was on and sometimes it wasn't, or it might have been but we were both in our own little worlds and didn't really notice either way. We'd take back roads so we could escape the busyness of the city, free from having to stop for traffic, instead almost as if we were just floating on our journey. I'd do most of my daydreaming then. Occasionally he'd ask me a question and I'd be so caught up in my thoughts that I would randomly answer, never really knowing what it was he had just asked. I loved those drives with him and still do. He'll come by my place for a visit and we'll end up grabbing a coffee and randomly drive while catching up.

Some women like to shop or go for manicures, I on the other hand would rather spend money on the gas and just get out and drive. It's a huge stress reliever for me - getting out on those back roads that my dad and I used to take and to let my mind wander. My mood usually dictates the music I need to listen to and many times I have the same song playing on repeat. I'm gone for 45 mins on average but could probably go for a couple hours. I love being still in thought but yet my fidgety self needs to be moving, it's a perfect combination.

I love spending time with my children and that means I share with them the experience of driving aimlessly as I did with my Father. I'll call them by their own nicknames, "Bubby or Luvie", pile them in the car, go grab a coffee for myself and some TimBits for them and then head out for the freedom of the road. At first there's lots of commotion going on, fighting about which songs will be played or whether one child looked at the other in a rude manner, typical brother/sister nonsense until they get into the "zone". That perfect moment when I realize all I can hear is the music and the quiet hum of the engine. I look in the rear view mirror to see them sitting back, gazing out their own windows and clearly they're daydreaming just as I used to at their age. It's those moments that I literally take snapshots with my eyes and reminisce about later on. Peaceful moments that the three of us are together and yet also on our own.

The three of us. Just us three.

My dad is my hero and his divorce from my mother never diminished that for me. I hope my children will have warm memories of these drives and maybe even pass them onto their own children...most importantly, I hope they know I tried my best at being their Mother and forgive me for not being able to make it work with their father.

Daith Hardd

Finding Home

October 1, 2013

So the ball is rolling in finding a place of my own, with my two children. It's all a bit daunting as I've never actually lived on my own. I was 19 when I moved out from my Father's home to a basement apartment with my husband in Oakville, Ontario. He was attending Sheridan college and I was working in the city. When we did move back to our hometown of Oshawa, we rented a room with a bunch of guys that we had known from high school. I might add that those few months with all of us living under the same roof were some of the best times/memories/life experiences I've ever had. I've never lived with other women before, but from the stories I have heard, men are much more flexible and easier to get along with…at least from my experience.

My needs/wants for this place aren't extensive. A home, close to their school and their father, preferably in the same neighbourhood and within my limited budget are what I NEED. What I want is much more flexible. Clean, three bedrooms and not a lot of grass to cut!

I can barely dress myself stylishly, let alone try and decorate a house so this will be a work in progress. First and foremost will be getting the children happy and settled into their own bedroom and then the three of us will figure out the rest. I have decided on one thing though.

At work I send out a daily email of motivation or a positive affirmation. It helps to start the day off right and at least one person from my distribution list always comments back to say how that certain message really helped put them in a good mood. It's something simple that I enjoy doing and I love sharing them with others. Over the course of time, I have collected an extensive amount of motivational artwork that I am now going to put to great use. I plan on going through the lot of them, printing them off, framing them and displaying them on one fabulous wall in my home. A special place that as soon as I walk in my front door, those motivational, positive quotes shout out at me and fill me with joy. Simple pleasures, am I right?

There are so many things that I could spend my time being bitter and angry about during this huge change in my life but I'm not going to give it the time of day. I have so much to be thankful for and I'd rather spend my time celebrating all these fabulous things.

Life is to be enjoyed, not just endured.

Daith Hardd

Do I Turn You Off?

October 7, 2013

"I like intelligent women. When you go out, it shouldn't be a staring contest." ~Frank Sinatra

How many men are attracted to intelligent women who have an informed opinion? Maybe it's just my own insecurities but whenever I start to express my desires for an educated conversation or an interest in a typically male subject, I feel like I should back off. That if I really want to find a significant other, I'll have to compromise this vital part of my being. My true identity.

Maybe I don't fit into the "typical" female mould? I don't enjoy cooking or baking, nor do I like to do knitting or other crafty hobbies. Pretty coloured nails or high heel shoes have never been a passion of mine, in fact I really don't enjoy shopping or putting together stylish outfits either. I think the closest I actually get to being feminine is putting on makeup, shaving my legs and generally smelling good (thanks to the patchouli scent of Karma from Lush cosmetics). Other than that, I'm really a rather goofy and nerdy gal.

I've said it before and I'll say it again, I'm a sapiophile. I'm most attracted to intelligent and unique men. Someone who is open to other points of views and the never ending quest for knowledge. I don't care if you have money, or a fancy job title or GQ good looks, because that's not what attracts me to you.

All that can be lost in a blink of eye.

So maybe I need to get over my own insecurities. Maybe I need to rethink what men want and know that the right man will want me for exactly who I am. Intelligent, inquisitive, goofy and unique.

If you're out there, so am I.

Daith Hardd

Be Happy. Love Life

October 9, 2013

I know this is a recurring theme of mine with my blog, but I speak the truth. We can only control so much in our lives and the rest isn't up to us. We can't control what other people will do to us, or the other bumps in the road, but what we can control is our outlook and how we react to these events.

I had my life planned out when I was 23. I wanted to be a wife and stay at home mother/nurturer. I spent years focusing on and encouraging my husband with his career and I was happy doing it. We were a great team, best of friends and I truly believed we would grow old together. That was the plan. That was our financial plan as well and we worked hard to do the appropriate things to make retirement together not only comfortable but enjoyable. But bumps occurred and then huge pot holes.

My life is starting over. I'm out on my own and instead of feeling sorry for myself and bitter about what has happened, I've chosen to move forward. To be thankful for everything else that I do have.

Be bitter or be better… one of the greatest pieces of advice I was ever given and I think of it often. You can choose the same in your very own life. Be better. Be happy. Love life.

Daith Hardd

I Am Complete

October 11, 2013

There's nothing wrong with being alone, in fact before you can even consider sharing yourself with another, you need to be happy just as you are. In your own company, in your own skin. You can't step into a relationship with the fairy tale expectation that that person will complete you. Instead, they should be viewed as a compliment. A beautiful coupling of two complete human beings.

When I left my marriage, this was the discussion I had with myself: stay and be lonely or leave and be complete. I knew there was a possibility that I might not ever find another person to share my life with, and although this deeply saddened me, I knew I was whole, just as is. I love myself. I love the woman I have become. I love my life and it's perfect just as it is.

I'm ready to share myself with another complete soul but I'm cautious not to lose who I am in the process. Relationships can be a roller coaster of emotions. With the delirious upswing of lust and love, come the terrible dips of sadness and despair if things don't work out. I'm cautious about getting on this ride, but I know that it's part and parcel with the process. I won't lose sight of myself and if/when things don't work out, I'll be able to dust myself off and keep going…

Because I'm complete with or without a man.

Daith Hardd

Why I Do This Blog

October 16, 2013

"Think twice before you speak, because your words and influence will plant the seed of either success or failure in the mind of another."

~ Napoleon Hill

The original premise for this blog was to document an experiment I was doing, for myself and for my children. I created Corff Hardd (Body Beautiful in Welsh) to explore what truly makes us beautiful from the inside out. During this time, I refrained from looking into a mirror or any reflection of myself for 30 days as well as not wearing any make-up. I wanted to pull out my confidence from the inside rather than standing on the belief that who I was, was only visible from the outside and I wanted to share this experience with my children. It was important for me that they be able to look up to me as a strong, confident woman, Mother and role model. Almost daily I would post about different topics regarding what true beauty was, doing research on different cultures or social media, and I would bring these subjects up carefully for discussion with my children. When the 30 days were complete, I realized I still had a lot to learn about life, love and being a good role model for my children, so I created this sister blog Daith Hardd or Beautiful Journey in Welsh.

Looking back just 12 months from today, I have seen a lot of positive change in my life. I no longer take a back seat to the journey that is my life. I am in control of what I want and don't want out of it. I'm confident in my abilities and I am proud of all that I have accomplished, because in these 12 months I have accomplished a lot! Most importantly, I am a strong woman who is equal to any man out there. This is what I will pass on to my children.

My daughter will learn that brains and not beauty are far more fulfilling to a woman's soul. That she has the right to an opinion and to be heard just as equally as any man. In order to give unconditional love to another human being, she will also have to do so with herself. She will have compassion but that it won't ever be mistaken for weakness. She will be brave woman.

My son will treat all women with respect and equality. He will know that the true essence of a woman can only be found through patience and love. That admitting his mistakes is not a sign of weakness nor is being vulnerable a slight against his manhood. He will be a remarkable man.

I am so proud to be the mother of these incredible children. Everyday, they teach me how important my role is in shaping their lives into being great, loving, compassionate and strong individuals.

Life is a beautiful journey,

Daith Hardd

Divorce is Not a Dirty Word

October 30, 2013

There's a social change that's been happening for years. Marital separation and divorce are now considered the norm and no longer part of the minority. Should we encourage couples to work through the difficulties that arise in relationships? Absolutely, but I no longer think we need to revere those who make it to those magical milestone years. There is no badge or trophy at the end if you simply endure a marriage for the sake of saving face. Remain in a marriage for the right reasons – because you love sharing your life with that partner.

Maybe I can say all this because I was married to my best friend for 10 years. I used to view the word divorce as a sign of failure, that a couple simply threw in the towel when the going got tough. Thankfully, I'm much wiser now. I know how hard it is to keep a pulse in an already dead relationship and I also know how much courage it takes to finally admit when it's over. We ended our marriage as friends and thankfully, not enemies.

If you're staying because you don't want to become one of the "statistics", take a look around and realize statistics are everywhere and you'd be best to be a happy one.

Daith Hardd

You're Invited To a Pity Party

November 6, 2013

Yada yada yada...

I'm conscious when I write sad and depressing posts that I may also be dragging others down with me. The whole pity party blogs have always irked me. I realize this probably makes me sound like a real jerk, and maybe I am, but at least I'm being honest. I always have the decision to just not read what the blogger has posted, as do you. So if you're fed up with me moaning and groaning about my life, please don't waste your time reading on...because this really isn't about you, it's about me. My trials and tribulations and for me, blogging is very cheap therapy.

I'm busier than ever both professionally and personally. I figure the more I distract myself the easier it is to not think about what's happening in my life. Every moment of my day is filled with something that needs to be done, completed and sorted out until the time comes to put the children to bed and I crash with them. If I still have things that need to be finished, I'll wake up around midnight and get it all done. I just need to keep forging ahead. At times it almost feels as though I'm in labour, painful as hell but knowing at the end of it there will be some fantastic reward.

I've had a few really bad days though. Days where I could barely get out of bed and into work. Days where I've sat at my desk and secretly cried. Days where I just didn't want to go home and face my children. Days where I could describe to you in detail what the pain feels, tastes and looks like.

I wish there was a miracle cure so that I could just skip this whole process and go back to feeling my regular, happy-go-lucky self.

I want off this roller coaster ride. I'm exhausted. I want to scream and pound my fists into the wall until they bleed. That physical release...but like I said, I'm just too exhausted.

In the end, I'm no different that any other blogger on here trying to find their way in life. Navigating through all the bullshit. So the next time I read someone's post about how down and out they are, I'll have a bit more compassion. I'll either read it or turn the page. That's always your choice as well.

If you've made it to the end of this post, thank you...for listening.

Daith Hardd

Love-able

November 13, 2013

As much as I have confidence in myself, those awful worries creep into my thoughts. The fear that something is unloveable about me. If the one man that I loved with all my might couldn't love me in the way that a husband should, why would anyone else want to? I ask this question so often that it hurts.

I've been lonely for so long and I'm terrified to put my heart out there for it to only result in rejection.

I want to be loved. I want to be a strong, confident woman who believes I am worthy of love.

Daith Hardd

Flee

November 15, 2013

I get in the car early in the morning and drive. Drive past my work, past my city boundaries, past all the hurt, pain and loneliness I feel.

There's a dirt road that leads to a dead end. A dead end like my life. Without even realizing it, I'm parked and walking toward the silent and solemn trees. I'm alone. All alone. My friends are like the trees around me, many but unable to help.

I've gone hoarse from screaming at the sky. Cursing the clouds and wishing the earth to swallow me. I'm an empty shell of who I once was. I'm not the strong oak tree that I portray to my children. I'm a woman just trying to survive for them.

I'll dig a hole and bury myself down deep to feel safe and secure. To feel as though I'm being held while my body shakes with sobs. Tears that become puddles of mud around me. Each drop that falls will take a tiny piece of my grief. How many tears must fall before I feel whole again? Drain and empty me in order to feel full?

I can't return home until I am firmly planted and growing into that strong oak tree.

Daith Hardd

Life: Not in Years but With Purpose

November 19, 2013

I'll live to a hundred and still never accomplish all that I wish to. I need to be reincarnated and lead a life multiple times over...each time vastly different than the last. For now, I'll dream.

I'll be a nomad. No home to call my own but the open space of land with which I will roam. Everyday I'll awake and set out for a new place to rest and by rest I mean to sing as loudly as I like, dance and be as foolish as I can be. In my pockets there will always be pencil and some sort of parchment with which to write the lyrics of my ballads. At night I'll never be lonely. Laying underneath a blanket of stars will give me all the company I need and desire.

When I've become tired of having conversations with myself, I'll seek out others. A community of people who will have a common goal as I, to love and be loved. They will be my family. There will be no more silence, instead a comforting hum of friends coming and goings. We will live under one roof, eat and pray together and cherish one another. Loneliness will never creep in.

I'll clone myself into millions of mini Jenn's. Each of them will have a purpose. Some will be healers. They will fold you into their arms, holding you close and absorbing the pain you feel. Their eyes will look into your soul and you'll instantly know you are loved, no strings attached, no judgement. Simple, true, love.

Other mini Jenn's will go out and live by the simple rules of life...do good and be good. Helping others. Leave all possessions behind and be paid in the knowledge that my minions eased burdens and hardships. Their moral compass will flow to everyone that they encounter. Honesty, integrity, compassion and love will be just a few of the character traits given freely to others.

I'll love more than I've ever loved before, yet I won't fall in love. The goodness of my soul will be on my sleeve, not on my face. My beauty will not be seen, it will be felt. I'll stretch my legs and run, never stopping for rest.

Daith Hardd

This Morning…

November 21, 2013

This morning...

I wanted to dissolve into my mattress. The weight of my sorrow heavier than the body with which it held. Each exhale bringing me closer to no longer existing.

This morning...

I wanted to float above my body. Escape from the torture that has kept me in captivity. Gazing down upon my shell, I would only feel tranquil, peaceful and rested.

This morning...

I took one step, then another and another. I tripped, bled and sobbed...hard and long but I stood back up and kept walking.

This morning, I survived.

Daith Hardd

Friends or Lovers?

November 30, 2013

You have a choice. Behind door number 1 is the potential love of your life and behind door number 2 are your best platonic friends. Which would you choose?

If you choose the first door you will have a soulmate. Someone who has the potential to love you more than you thought possible. To connect with in the most intimate, physical ways that two lovers can. They also have the ability to break your heart and make you buckle at the knees in despair.

Yet if you choose the second door you will have friendships. Not just one, but many people who will love you and be your companion. Deep love and contentment but no passion. No spark.

Which door would you choose?

Daith Hardd

Just Be Perfect?

December 1, 2013

It isn't working.

Shoving down those dark thoughts about myself and covering them with Just-Be-Perfect. Just-Be-Selfless. Just-Think-Good-Thoughts. Because if you don't do these things, people won't like you.

I finally had the "A-ha" moment. I realize that I do all these distraction methods in order to ensure I'm never not liked, which I realize is impossible - but then again, I obviously don't since I keep doing these things.

It seems to work well if I keep myself in a little bubble where I don't let someone truly know me. I'll just give little tid bits of myself. Because if I'm kind and good then I won't have to worry about rejection. Right?

I'll hide the rest because the rest isn't worth loving. There's something hideous inside of me that even I don't know what it is. If I allow this tiny bit of me out, men will run and hide. Isn't that what happened with my marriage? If he couldn't love me then what chance is there of anyone else?

I guess until I sort this mess out, I can't move forward with much else.

Daith Hardd

Earning My Sea Legs

December 5, 2013

In order to move forward you need to put one foot ahead of the other and keep going. At first it's a crawl but eventually you're on your feet and standing. I feel as though I am getting my sea legs, I'm really wobbly but I know it will pass. Practice makes perfect and that's where I'm at…practicing this whole opening up my heart to another.

Like I said, I'm at the beginning stages and that's the only way to start. I can feel those moments of happiness and I'm holding fast and hard to them. It's absolutely terrifying though. Opening up when I just want to shut down, hide and protect my heart. Keep them at a distance so that they don't know how to hurt you and yet, I'm intrigued enough to at least try.

Little tiny bits though, that's all I can give at the moment because I still feel very fragile.

Be bold and get moving until your running wild and carefree.

Daith Hardd

The Gift of Hope

December 13, 2013

Daith Hardd – Beautiful Journey, it still is.

So I dipped my toes into the lake of love and pulled back too quickly. It was warm and inviting and exactly what my heart needed and yet apparently not what I was ready for. My fear propelled me to think the worst instead of the proof that was before me. I didn't give them the benefit of the doubt which in turn has taught me another life lesson.

Surprising myself, I'm actually ok. I thought when something like this were to happen, I'd be a right mess. That I'd have to start back from square one. Maybe there is growth happening inside of me? Maybe I actually took 10 leaps forward and only 2 steps back.

Maybe I can be thankful for the chance to have rubbed shoulders with another good and honest soul...I learned this a tad bit too late.

During my darkest hours I played an album on repeat. Every song hit a raw nerve that gave me the allowance I needed to mourn and grieve what once was. I needed something that would help draw out all the pain that I had bottled up inside of myself for so long. It was a painfully beautiful experience. I played that same album this morning, expecting to relive those same emotions but I didn't. My heart fluttered a bit and instead of sadness, I felt the faint but very obvious sense of hope.

A few bumps and bruises but still going hard.

It's a Daith Hardd.

Twitter

December 11, 2013

This is just a quick post for those of you that have followed me via Twitter.

First of all, thank you. I don't know who you are and why at times you even want to read my blog but I take it as a compliment. I don't actually follow that many people on Twitter simply because I can't juggle or have any kind of connection if my numbers get too high. That's really what I enjoy about Twitter, connecting with people that you may never have had a chance to otherwise.

I like being accessible and open about my life. I don't mind answering personal questions because there have been plenty of time where I've asked you them as well. I guess this brings me to my next chapter in life. I'm still going to be open and honest with my life's journey but I've decided to keep it a bit more private. I'd like a significant other to make their opinions about me not by what they have read via Twitter or my blog, but the good old fashion way.

So if you had been wondering why the blog link was removed from twitter, rest assured it's nothing personal…but at the same time, it is

Daith Hardd

This Is Good

December 14, 2013

I've been down and out as of lately and not able to write much of the uplifting stuff I usually like to. You can't force yourself to feel something that just isn't there and so I haven't.

Today feels different.

It feels hopeful.

My mouth is beginning to turn upward into a smile. This is good.

I'm a very reflective person and I examine myself/life often. Wondering at the progress I'm making, if I'm actually making any at all. I am though. This past week I've mulled over a lot and realized I'm making huge gains. I'm no longer falling flat on my face when I trip…I'm actually staying upright. The pain isn't as raw or at the surface, bubbling over either. I think I might actually give myself permission to allow someone to love me.

Love isn't here, yet… YET. But it will come. I'm sure of it.

I'm smiling now. This is good.

Daith Hardd

We Need One Another

December 14, 2013

You are out there. Maybe a thousand miles away, but you are and you're searching for me too. Distance won't matter. Believe this.

I won't settle for anything less than having you. I'm older, more mature and I know exactly what this big heart of mine needs. It needs you and you need me. We need each other. Simple as that.

I'll be patient, as hard as that may be, but I will. I'll wait years if need. There's really no choice in the matter because my heart belongs to you. It probably always has. You can try and sort out life without me, run, hide, bury yourself in the busyness of life but we will find one another.

I can make the best of anything. I've done it my entire life but I won't do it this time. I refuse. I adamantly refuse. I'm tired of feeling cheated in love when I have so much of it to give.

There will be others I'll be able to share a comfortable existence with, but that's not what I"m searching for. I'm searching for you.

And you are searching for me.

Daith Hardd

Swimming to Shore

December 19, 2013

You don't really know what kind of person you are until you're put in the position to either sink or swim. I always thought I'd be the one to sink. Although I masked it pretty well, I didn't have a lot of self confidence. I took a backseat in my life's journey. Went with the flow and really didn't have much of a direction as to where I was heading.

I tried to stay positive through it all. I told myself each year it was going to get better. Since having my son in 2007 it's been more than a struggle. Within minutes of his birth I experienced a very traumatic and terrifying surgery which forever changed my life. These health issues have since taken a toll on my body and my personal life and I've had to give up on the dream of having more children.

Maybe this was the beginning of the demise of my marriage or maybe we just grew apart. Maybe we just married too young. Maybe this or maybe that…who cares about it anymore. It is what it is, and I'd like to think we're both happy to move on as friends rather than remain as spouses.

We're both guilty of hurting one another - whether it was intentional or not - and I'm ready to shoulder some of that burden. He's been my best friend for over 16 years and although I blamed him for trying to sink my ship, I've seen him try and repair it.

He didn't save me, I saved myself and I swam to shore…I'd like to think he's proud of me for that….Daith Hardd

CHAPTER THREE

Rebirth

Signed, Sealed, Delivered...No Longer Yours

December 27, 2013

1pm

This is the time that I officially signed off on my separation paperwork, enabling me to start my life's next chapter. I'm leaving this house in the New Year and moving into the home that I will share with our children.

My home. My place. Mine.

Through mediation, we sifted through all our finances, custody arrangements and property division ... that which took 16 years to accumulate, sorted in a matter of hours. During the process it never occurred to either of us not be honest and fair to one another. We both have equally won/lost this marriage. There are no winners at the end of the day...yet there is a sense of relief. We survived THIS and we have remained friends...in fact, best of platonic friends, which I always dismissed as impossible.

I'm ok. I don't have regrets. But I do feel like being a bit cynical tonight, talking filthy with friends and getting more than a little tipsy.

Papers have been signed, sealed and delivered...just no longer yours.

Daith Hardd

My Ex, My Friend

January 11, 2014

I had no idea what to expect, telling the children that their father and I were separating. Lily has always been my more sensitive child, filled with anxiety on a daily basis, seeing a psychologist every week. Jonah on the other hand, has always been a free spirit, laughing, making jokes and popular with other children. I've never had to fret or worry over him.

We did our homework and spoke with Lily's psychologist who explained that the best time to tell the children would be a couple weeks before the move. It would be best not to give them too much time to brood over things. The children and I are moving at the end of the month to a home of our own, just around the corner from where we are now so we decided to break the news to them last night.

We had an easy meal of pizza and then cuddled them on the couch to give the news. Marcus did a great job at explaining that although we both still loved one another, our love had changed and that we would be separating. He told them the standard stuff that you tell children at these times. That we loved them and that would never change. We would still be a family, just a little bit different. That they would live with me but see him all the time.

I caught him choking on his words, eyes welling with tears and having to pause to compose himself. He is an amazing father and it pains me to know he's drawn the short straw in this next chapter. He won't live with them, he won't see them everyday, tuck them into bed or sneak in for a quick kiss before he retires for the night. When the three of us leave, he'll be on his own in this big empty house with nothing but memories and beautiful BrownDog.

I spent the last few months worrying about how the children would take the news. I didn't have a moment to give thought on how Marcus was or would be handling all this. Now I do. Now I see how absolutely gutted he is over this and how I can't actually fix it for him.

He'll always be apart of my life, we have children and we have a great history together. We've moved past the pain we caused one another and found that being friends is the best for all of us.

He is my ex, but forever my friend.

Daith Hardd

She is Me

January 18, 2014

The big day has been set. Thursday, January 23 at 11am, years of careful thought and planning will be inked on my forearm. A beautiful piece of artwork that I've been wanting for years, celebrating who I am and who I have become.

I've admired women who've had the "balls" to display art on their body. It shows a certain amount of confidence in yourself when you just don't give a fuck what others think of it. It means something to you, a story about your life and you want to share it with others. It creates conversations, discussions and engages others in your life.

I remember my father always being critical of those with tattoos. He'd often tell me that for someone to do such a thing to their body, they must have some self hatred. Tortured souls who would inflict pain and ugliness to bodies. I couldn't wrap my head around his mentality. For me, it has always been an expression of art. They loved their bodies so much they wanted to enhance it with a story. There was no self hatred in that. In fact, an incredible amount of love and appreciation for themselves. I've waited many years to find the right story to be created on my flesh.

I love women. I'm surrounded by incredibly strong women some of which don't even know their own strength. We all have our demons, we lean on one another, support and then pick each other up. We are awesome and we get even more AWESOME as the years pass.

This is the story of a woman who has come into her own. Everyday becoming more and more confident in herself. No longer playing the underdog, wandering aimlessly through life. She's taking control of her destiny, her dreams and aspirations.

She is me.

Daith Hardd

Gifts to Yourself

January 27, 2014

I splurged this weekend. And by splurge I mean, I treated myself to something that I didn't need but simply wanted and it felt divine!

I'm not entirely comfortable with money, which may sound rather odd. I've always given it more power than it deserves. I scrimp and save, often feeling nervous when I do in fact spend it. I have no qualms about shopping at thrift stores or simply going without. Hand me down clothes for my children were always appreciated and in my new home (40yrs plus in age but new to me), I've been more than happy to buy second hand furniture. If it isn't something like food, shelter or clothing, it's a luxury.

I'm not fancy and I don't need fancy "things" to make me happy… or so I thought. This weekend proved me wrong. Buying nice things for yourself doesn't have to come with guilt or the feeling as though you don't deserve it. It can feel good. Make you feel special. I work hard for my money and I should allow myself to be treated occasionally with a WANT item and not strictly a NEED.

I'm giving myself permission to enjoy some of the finer things in life. This is good.

Daith Hardd

Memories

February 7, 2014

Over the past few years I've had to let go of a number of "things" in order to welcome in the new "life". The fluff or surface pleasures that give us a temporary feeling of happiness. Things that make life comfortable but don't actually amount to much or simply put, items that only money can buy.

Those are the "things" that I can resign myself to. The harder changes are the dynamics within the friends/family circle. Knowing that as much as you don't want to say goodbye, sometimes that is exactly what needs to be done. The beautiful part of this is being left with a parting gift. Memories. That's what I have. Wonderful, magical and happy memories. I don't ever have to lose those.

I read an article not too long ago about the age in which a child starts to remember or make memories that they will carry on into adulthood. The study concluded that at roughly the age of 7, a child's brain has reached the maturity in which what happens from then onward, they will be able to recall.

My children fell below this age group so I couldn't help but feel saddened by this news. What did this mean for my children? Would the only real memories they have be of their parents being apart? Would they never remember all the good times we had as a complete and whole family? Vacations, adventures, learning, cuddling…was it all in vain? God knows the struggles my marriage had were never something that our friends or family saw, let alone be felt by our children. We just slowly fell out of love and instead become best friends. Our family memories are cherished and the idea that the children may not remember those times weighed on me heavily.

But studies are simply that. Not set in stone and there are variables. Many in fact. So as I was sitting down with my 6 year old son the other day, looking over old photo's, we came across a picture of his father and I. It was taken on our high school prom night, both of us dressed up and looking young and dapper. My boy enjoyed looking at it and then said something sweet.

"You two make a great couple". I smiled and didn't need to say anything more.

Memories. He remembers us as a happy family. I'm taking this with me.

Daith Hardd

The Little Engine That Could

May 6, 2014

I'm ok.

I'm ok?

At least I think I am.

I still have those moments where I feel like an emotional train wreck, but they are few and far between now. I'm keeping busy, busier than I have been in years which is therapeutic in it's own way. It keeps my mind active and focused on more important things/others – the world doesn't revolve around Jenn and her marriage breakup.

Every Thursday I have a lunch date. Not with a male companion but with my therapist. Yes, I have a therapist. One that I don't feel guilty about sobbing in front of or repeating the same things over and over or showing my true, bitter self to…because I pay her to listen, and give me advice. She's the one person to whom I don't care if she likes me. I can simply be me. I can show her my flaws and then leave knowing it all stays there. She won't hold it against me.

She is safe.

I'm still always thinking. Wondering what it is I want. Do I want platonic love or romantic love? Do I have to choose right now? Can I simply live life and let the chips fall where they may?

I think I can…I think I am…I think I'm ok.

Daith Hardd

Awesome Mistakes

May 13, 2014

There's nothing like having a girlfriend when you need a shoulder to cry on, but what about our guy friends?

Guy friends want to solve our problems. They don't want to sit around listening to us gripe and complain without ever making headway. We can count on them to give it to us straight, not mince words or try and soften the blow. If they think we're being foolish, they'll come right out and say it. Need relationship advice? Go to your guy friends! What makes you think that your girlfriends can accurately tell you what it is your man is trying to say and what he needs? Men know men!

I've got a collection of guy friends. Platonic, male friendship. Yes, it can completely exist. We check in with one another, shoot the shit, trade recipes and generally chat about nothing in particular. But when I need a man's perspective on life or more specifically, my (lack of) love life, they're ready and willing to fill me in.

These past few months have been ridiculously difficult for me to find my way through. I've had so many questions that needed answering or advice that my girlfriends haven't been able to give me and I'm thankful I have cool guy friends. Just recently a guy I've known for a couple years but haven't talked much to, reached out and gave me some relationship advice that I found very amusing but also helpful. He also told me this:

"…you'll get to make all kinds of awesome mistakes"

I've never heard of a mistake being described as awesome, but he's completely right! Instead of me dissecting everything that went wrong with this or that, I should just embrace the experience and the awesomeness of it. Since he gave me this advice I've smiled a little bit more and laughed at the absurdity of it. God knows I have certainly made some awesome and fun mistakes! And for the most part, I'm having one hell of a fun time doing it.

Thanks Jason. You rock!

Daith Hardd

Sabbatical 2014

May 21, 2014

Well, it's that time of year again where I need to take a bit of a sabbatical from social media – my personal Twitter account being one of them. I tend to pile my plate pretty high with both work and personal obligations that by June I need to step back and take a bit of a breather. It's May and I'm almost on oxygen…therefor I think it's time.

Time to do a bit more reading.

Time to do a bit more walking.

Time to do a bit more self-exploration.

…and most importantly, time to concentrate on my children and my partner.

It's been a really incredible journey these past 12 months and I thank all of you for sharing it with me. I will continue to post here and if you ever want to reach me, please feel free to email me. It may take me a while, but I will reply :)

See you all again in July/August.

Daith Hardd

Aziz

May 26, 2014

I found stars tonight that weren't in the sky. They were right in front of me, just slightly West of my home. Some were like shooting stars whizzing by me on the highway, while others were in high-rises. I traveled through space and yet I was grounded by my tires.

I rolled down the windows, allowing my hair to take flight and the temperature to make it chilly as it blew against my face. Each time it touched my skin it reminded me of a cool satin pillowcase, silky and soft. The air was sweet with the scent of jasmine and I couldn't pinpoint where it was coming from but I loved it. I adored it. It made my heart smile and made the experience of the stars all that more magical.

I drove for nearly three hours and although I was alone in that car I felt as though I had all the company I needed. I don't have the answers to my life, or life in general but I do know that it is a journey. I cherish each moment that my heart beats and every person I have the opportunity to meet and share my time with.

I know a wonderful star who named me Aziz. His star is bursting with light and forever on the move like a shooting star. Everyone is drawn to his sparkle, the twinkle in his eyes, and you're thankful that you had the chance to gaze upon such beauty. Some stars are fixed and you can see them in the sky night after night, you always know where to find them. Yet other stars wander. You know that they're up there, you may not be able to pinpoint where, but simply knowing that they exist makes life so special. Those stars will never extinguish.

To live is to live. So simple, so true. Let your star shine.

Daith Hardd

AFTERWARD

The journey never truly ends. Everyday brings with it new life, new experiences and new struggles. Life isn't easy, but we have the choice to roll with the punches, laugh at ourselves and keep moving forward.

I've fallen madly in love with myself through these past 20 months and it's a beautiful feeling. The journey hasn't ended and I intend to continue to document it on my blog if you care to follow-up.

Thank you for taking the time to read my words. I hope it inspires you to go on your own Daith Hardd.

With love,

Aziz Jenn

PAGE 2

PAGE 3